ANCIENT WOMEN WHO EMPOWER

Celia M. Hastings

Illustrations by

Sarah VanderArk

ISBN 979-8-89345-084-2 (paperback)
ISBN 979-8-89345-085-9 (digital)

Christian Faith Publishing
832 Park Avenue
Meadville, PA 16335
www.christianfaithpublishing.com

Cover illustration by Sarah VanderArk portrays the author and illustrator as ancient women working together on this book.
Author photo on back cover by Jodell Danbert.

Printed in the United States of America

To
Miss Sarah,

for whom justice seems elusive,
and to all who have known injustice.

Contents

Preface

Soon after writing *The Undertaker's Wife* in 2005, I learned about the inhumanity and injustice of the US mass incarceration system. This racially disparate system has grown 500% since 1970 (800% for women) and is out of proportion to population growth and crime rate. Our country has 4% of the earth's people and 25% of its prisoners. With prisons operated by for-profit corporations, the system puts profits over people, and conditions in prisons have become more inhumane and less restorative.

The Innocence Project estimates at least 10% of those in prisons are innocent. Once inside, those incarcerated are vulnerable and find it difficult to be extricated from "the system" or receive humane treatment within it. Many have untreated mental illness and need "health care rather than handcuffs." But health care in prisons seems hard to come by.

If 10% of the country's 2 million prisoners are innocent, that means 200,000 people times an annual cost of $40,000—or at least $800 billion per year—is spent on injustice. It also means at least 200,000 people who have committed crimes are free to commit more crimes. It is difficult to estimate the true cost of injustice for those in prison, their families, communities, and country, but one can be sure it is enormous.

Within several years of learning about the injustice and inhumanity of the US prison system, someone close to me became incarcerated. It appeared that cost-effectiveness in the resolution of cases was more important than justice. Instead of thoroughly investigating cases or going to the expense of a jury trial, it seemed easier and less costly to find a weak link, someone most likely to cave under pressure, confess, or take a plea bargain. It is even legal for officials to lie in order to bring about such an outcome. In this way, as Aesop observed long ago, "We hang the ***petty thieves*** and appoint the great ones to public office."

While I was learning about systemic injustice in our country, I was also writing stories about ancient women who shaped the culture and faith into which Jesus was born. In ordinary moments and in times of crises, their decisions and actions changed the direction of a nation. As I worked with their stories, injustice met empowerment.

So I wondered: if I put their stories into a book with illustrations to inspire the imagination, might these ancient women still empower people and show us the way to transform injustice into blessings? As Mother Teresa said,

> I'm a little pencil in the hand of a writing God, who is sending a love letter to the world.

Acknowledgments

In writing about the ancient women on these pages, I am indebted to the well-organized and well-researched work of Edith Deen in *All the Women of the Bible*. It was her work that brought many of these women to my attention.

Earlier versions of these stories appeared some years ago in the *Petoskey News-Review*. The welcome responses I received were the seeds that grew the stories into a book.

I am grateful to artist Sarah VanderArk for the fresh and creative illustrations that brought the stories of the ancient women to life on these pages. Our collaboration has been insightful and fun.

Many thanks to the Christian Faith Publishing staff who fashioned my writing and Sarah's illustrations into a book. It wouldn't have happened without you!

Shepherding Women

Wisdom is the way
God shepherds us to Shalom.

—Celia M. Hastings
Theme of *A Bible Survey Curriculum for Adults*
(The Wisdom Series)

Sarai/Sarah

Gave Birth to Laughter

Genesis 11–25, Hebrews 11:11

Long, long ago, in a Middle Eastern area known as Ur, a wealthy and beautiful woman named Sarai lived with her half-brother/husband Abram—a common arrangement in ancient patriarchal culture. Sarai and Abram were shepherds who cared for sheep, goats, and camels. They also shepherded a large household of many people who worked for them.

Sarai and Abram knew the presence of the Holy One within themselves, in others, in the sheep and goats and camels, in the sunrises and sunsets, in the moon and stars, in the wind, in the fields, and in the heat of the day and the cool of the night. One day, as they communed with the Holy One, they received an amazing covenant of blessing: "I will make of you a great people. I will bless you and make your name so great that it will be used in blessings… And all the people on the face of the earth will be blessed through you."[1] The blessing included land and as many heirs as stars in the sky.

To enter into this blessing, Sarai and Abram had to leave their homeland and go on a long journey to a land they'd never seen. And so, by faith, Sarai and Abram, still childless at ages sixty-five and seventy-five, journeyed for hundreds of miles through wastelands and towns, moving at the pace of their lambs and pregnant ewes.

Sarai knew well the dangers of nomadic life for women. Ancient kings in the areas they traveled through often used cruelty and violence to gain women for their harems. Twice Sarai was taken into kings' harems because Abram said she was his sister—a half-truth. But each time, Sarai so gracefully conveyed she was also Abram's wife that, instead of starting a war or killing Abram, the kings gave him expensive gifts.

Although Sarai believed the Holy One's promise of heirs, she lived in a time and culture when barrenness was considered a divine curse. Meanwhile, pregnancy and childbirth were considered divine blessings and assurance of one's eternal destiny—which, in ancient times, meant living on through one's heirs.

Eleven years after leaving their homeland and trusting the Holy One's promise of heirs, Sarai and Abram still had no children. Most women her age were already great-grandmothers. So Sarai wondered. Perhaps the Holy One wanted her to do what was within her power to do. If she gave her maid Hagar to Abram as a concubine, any children born of this relationship would legally be Sarai's. Sarai did so, and Hagar gave birth to Ishmael, who was legally Sarai's son. But when Hagar treated Sarai badly because she was still barren, Sarai regretted her decision and made the painful choice to send Hagar and Ishmael away.

In time, the Holy One repeated the promise of heirs to Sarai and Abram. Sarai's name was changed from Sarai, as in the name of a barren mountain, to Sarah, meaning "Noblewoman."[2] Abram's name, meaning "Respected Parent," was changed to Abraham, meaning "Progenitor of a Multitude."[3]

More time passed. When Sarah was eighty-nine and no longer had her periods, three strangers visited their home. Sarah overheard their prediction that she would have a child within a year, and she chuckled to herself. "Now that I am so old and my husband even older, is pleasure to come my way again?"[4] The visitors heard her laughter and asked, "Is anything too extraordinary for God to do?"[5]

A year after the strangers' visit, when Sarah was ninety and Abraham was one hundred, Sarah gave birth to Isaac, whose name means "laughter."

As she nursed "Laughter," ninety-year-old Sarah remembered her life in Ur, the blessed promise, the call to leave, the dangerous journey through foreign lands, the long wait for heirs, and the time she had grown impatient in waiting. As she looked back, she had compassion for herself. She knew she was far more important to the Holy One than her weakest moments. So she laughed. "Now the Holy One has given me laughter, and all who hear of this will laugh with me."[6]

Sarah lived with laughter, gratitude, and joy for thirty-seven years after giving birth to Isaac. She died at the age of 127.

For Reflection or Discussion

1. Recall a time you may have felt impatient or been in a place you didn't want to be. How does one decide when to act and when to wait?
2. How might knowing you are far more important to the Holy One than your weakest moments help in your decision-making?
3. After making a decision one later regrets, how does one find compassion for oneself?
4. How might the difficult times of life seem when one is 90? Or 127?
5. How might one give birth to laughter?

Hagar

Saw and Heard the Holy One

Genesis 16, 21, 25

"Hagar, attendant of Sarai, where have you come from, and where are you going?"[7] asked the angel.

"I am running away from Sarai,"[8] Hagar replied.

Hagar of Egypt was working as an attendant to Sarai in a nomadic shepherding family. Her mistress, Sarai, who was barren, asked Hagar to have relations with Abram and bear a child who would legally belong to Sarai—a secondary-wife custom common in patriarchal times. But after

Hagar became pregnant, tensions arose between the women. Hagar felt so badly treated that she ran away into the desert and sat down by a spring on the road to Shur.

"You are now pregnant and you will bear a child; you will name it Ishmael—'God hears'—for God has heard you in your sorrow,"[9] the angel said. "Go back to Sarai and submit to her. I will make your descendants too numerous to count."[10]

Hagar recognized who spoke to her and was amazed that she had seen and heard the Holy One and was still alive. That is why the well is called Well of the Living One Who Sees Me.[11]

Hagar returned to Sarai and Abram, and when her child was born, Abram named him Ishmael. When Ishmael was thirteen, he and Abram and all the males of the household were circumcised, a sign of their inclusion in a covenant of blessing with the Holy One. The Holy One promised to bless Ishmael with a family of twelve leaders and make them into a great nation.

That same year, when baby Isaac was born to aged Sarah and Abraham, Hagar and Ishmael were sent away with a supply of bread and water. When the supply of water was gone, Hagar put Ishmael under a bush and sat down some distance away so she would not have to watch her child die. She began to weep.

Again, the angel spoke to her. "What is wrong, Hagar? … Do not be afraid, for God has heard the child's cry. Get up, lift up the child and hold his hand; for I will make of him a great nation."[12] Hagar looked up and saw a well, got some water, and gave Ishmael a drink.

True to the Holy One's promise, Ishmael thrived and became a fine archer. Abraham provided for him and Hagar, and when Abraham died, Ishmael joined Isaac to bury their father. As promised, Hagar's son, Ishmael, married and became the father of twelve tribal leaders who became a great nation. Some believe that it is from the Arabs of the Hagar–Abraham line that the prophet Muhammad descended and that Hagar is the mother of Islam.

For Reflection or Discussion

1. Have you known a time you wanted to run away?
2. How does one decide when to stay and when to go?
3. How can one see and hear the Holy One in difficult times?

Rebecca

Shepherd of the Covenant

Genesis 24–27

Rebecca was a shepherd who lived in Mesopotamia, where she and her brother, Laban, cared for the family's sheep and cattle and camels. Shepherding was hard work, but Rebecca was strong for the tasks. She drew water from the well in the morning, noon, and evening along with other women who drew water for their families and herds.

One evening, when Rebecca was drawing water, a tired elderly man asked her for a drink. She gave him water and said, "Drink, sir."[13] When she saw the ten camels kneeling beside him, she said, "I'll draw water for your camels until they have had their fill."[14] This was no small task since camels drink a lot of water and store it for desert travel.

After the camels drank their fill, the man told Rebecca her kindness had shown him she was the one his master Abraham wished to become Isaac's wife. The man gave her a gold nose ring and two gold bracelets.

With her family's blessing, Rebecca left her home-land and made the long journey by caravan. As the caravan approached her new home, she saw Isaac running toward them. She loved him from the moment they met, and they were married.

Although Rebecca and Isaac were very much in love, Rebecca was barren for twenty years. Their prayers for children were answered when she became pregnant with twins. The twins jostled each other within her womb, and she found the turmoil deeply disturbing. She said, "If this is the way it is to be, why go on living?"[15] Rebecca asked for divine guidance, and the Holy One told her, "Two nations are in your womb, two tribes in your belly who will be rivals. One will be stronger than the other, and the older will serve the younger."[16]

Rebecca kept this answer in her heart as she watched her twin sons grow. Esau, the firstborn, was a rugged outdoors-man and skillful hunter. He was the favorite of Isaac, who had a taste for wild game. Jacob was the quiet one who stayed among the tents and cooked. Rebecca noticed how much he cherished the Holy One's covenant and blessings.

Rebecca knew that one day when Esau was very hungry, he had traded his firstborn birthright for some stew Jacob had cooked. She also noticed that Esau showed little regard for the ethnic separation, which was an early-stage condition of the covenant. He had married two Hittite women, who were a source of grief to Rebecca and Isaac.

Rebecca remembered the Holy One's words that the elder would serve the younger. She understood why, and she knew what she had to do. One day, when Isaac was old and blind and dying, Rebecca overheard him preparing to give Esau the blessing of the firstborn, which Esau had earlier traded away. So she contrived a plan to help Jacob deceive Isaac and receive the blessing of the firstborn.

When Esau found out Jacob had received the blessing of the firstborn, he planned to kill Jacob. Rebecca again knew what she needed to do to preserve the covenant. She sent Jacob far away to her brother's family, knowing she would probably not live to see him again.

With insight, strength, and courage, Rebecca shepherded the Holy One's covenant through the ups and downs of sibling rivalry. She entrusted the covenant to the son who honored it. Like her mother-in-law, Sarah, Rebecca became a mother of nations.

In spite of the brotherly turmoil, readers are told Jacob and Esau eventually reconciled. Both of Rebecca and Isaac's children were blessed and became great nations.

For Reflection or Discussion

1. Was there a time you wondered, "If this is the way it's going to be, why go on living?" or asked, "Why is this happening to me?"
2. How might one access wisdom within, as well as strength and courage, in times like these?
3. What difficult choices may need to be made in order to move forward?

Leah and Rachel
Shepherds Who Built a Nation

Genesis 29–35

Leah and Rachel were sisters in the fields, tending sheep, when their cousin Jacob came to stay with their family. Rachel and Jacob soon fell in love and wanted to marry, but because Jacob had come from far away and had no riches to offer, Rachel's father, Laban, would agree to the marriage only if Jacob served as a shepherd for seven years.

At the end of seven years, Laban deceived Jacob by giving his eldest daughter, Leah, in marriage. Rachel was also given in marriage on the condition that Jacob serve Laban another seven years.

Leah bore children, but Rachel was barren. Being barren was difficult for her because in their culture, pregnancy and childbirth were regarded as encounters with the Holy One. In time, however, she did have a child. Leah and Rachel grew closer as sisters, wives, and mothers, while Jacob worked for Laban, provided well, and built wealth for the family in flocks and herds.

Leah and Rachel were aware of the many ways their father deceived Jacob and took advantage of him. After their father had changed Jacob's wages ten times, Leah and Rachel met with Jacob and spoke up. "We no longer have an inheritance in our father's house. Aren't we regarded as foreigners, now that he has effectively sold us and used up the purchase price?"[17]

So Rachel and Leah, with maids Bilhah and Zilpah, and husband Jacob gathered their children and flocks and herds and headed toward Jacob's homeland. When Laban pursued them, Leah and Rachel stood firmly against their father's anger until he kissed them and blessed them on their way.

By speaking up and standing up for truth and justice, Leah and Rachel became the shepherd-mothers of the twelve tribal leaders of a great nation.

For Reflection or Discussion

1. Recall a time you may have experienced someone's injustice or anger.
2. How does one know when to stay or when to move on?
3. How does one know how and when to speak up and stand up for truth and justice?

Women of the
Royal Line

**THIS IS THE FAMILY RECORD
OF JESUS THE CHRIST...**

Tamar and Judah begot
Perez and Zerah...
Rahab and Salmon begot Boaz;
Ruth and Boaz begot Obed...
Bathsheba—who had been the wife of
Uriah—and David begot Solomon...

—Matthew 1:1–6 The Inclusive Bible

Tamar

Gave Birth to the Royal Line

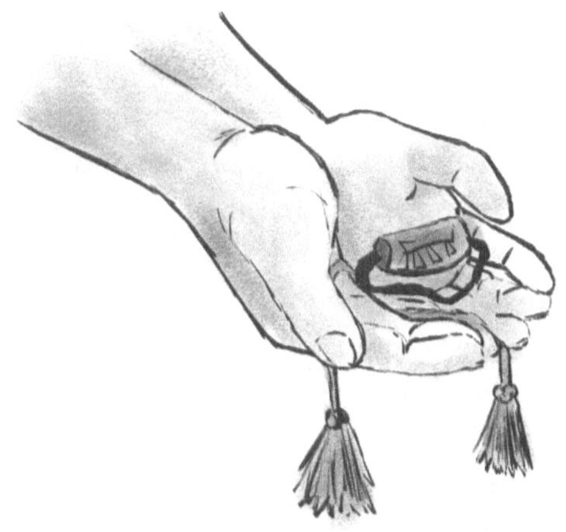

Genesis 38, Matthew 1:3

Tamar took off her widow's clothing, covered herself with a prostitute's veil, and sat by the roadside. Her father-in-law, Judah, son of Jacob, didn't recognize her and asked, "Let me lie with you."[18]

"What will you give me in return?"[19] Tamar asked.

"I will send you a young goat from my herd,"[20] he promised.

Tamar asked for a pledge until the goat was sent: "Your seal, its cord, and the staff in your hand."[21]

When Judah provided the pledge, she slept with him. Afterward, she returned home, took off the prostitute's veil, and wore her widow's clothing.

Tamar had been married to Judah's son Er. After Er died, his brother Onan married Tamar to fulfill the levirate law and produce an heir in Er's name. But Onan reneged on his duty and died also. Judah sent Tamar to live in her father's home until Judah's remaining son, Shelah, came of age and could marry her. But when Shelah came of age, Judah delayed the promised marriage—a great injustice to Tamar.

Tamar was keenly aware that in the sacred covenant, one's legacy and inheritance of land depended on having heirs. But Judah, the widowed son of the patriarch Jacob/Israel, seemed unaware and unconcerned. Tamar was not willing to let his indifference and injustice determine her fate. She followed her inner truth.

Three months after the roadside encounter, word reached Judah that his widowed daughter-in-law, Tamar, was pregnant from prostitution. As the law required, he ordered, "Bring her out! Let her be burned to death."[22]

When Tamar arrived, she displayed Judah's seal, cord, and staff and said, "I am pregnant by the man who owns these."[23] And Judah conceded. "She is more in the right than I."[24]

Tamar gave birth to twins, Perez and Zerah. Perez became head of a leading clan of Judah. In this way, Tamar became the matriarch of the royal tribal line of Judah.

When Tamar was sidelined and forgotten by the religious culture around her, she risked her life to follow eternal truth and justice. Within her womb, she transformed an injustice into a blessing and redeemed her husband's and father-in-law's legacy.

Tamar's wisdom continues to bless women who experience the spiritual indifference and injustice of others.

For Reflection or Discussion

1. Recall a time you may have experienced the spiritual indifference or injustice of others.
2. What do you have in your hands that may transform this indifference and injustice into a blessing?
3. How may your decisions and actions affect future generations?

Rahab

Innkeeper with a Rooftop Secret

Joshua 2 and 6, Matthew 1:5, Hebrews 11:11

The Jericho police pounded on Rahab's door. "Bring me the two who are lodging in your house, for they are here to spy on my land."[25]

Rahab was an innkeeper whose house was perched atop the double walls of the City of Palms. Her house had a strategic view of the area west of the Jordan River.

Rahab knew the people of Jericho were on edge. The Hebrew tribes had camped east of the Jordan River and were coming to reclaim the land of their ancestors. Jericho was the gateway to that land. Jericho's people also knew of the Holy One who had delivered the Hebrew people from their oppressors, led them through the Sea of Reeds on dry ground, and given them manna and water in the wilderness.

Rahab knew the Holy One of the Hebrew people was real and true and powerful. So she told the police, "Yes, they did come here… they left. I don't know where they went. But you might catch up to them if you hurry."[26]

When the police were out of sight, she went to her rooftop, where she had hidden the Hebrew spies under stalks of flax she was drying. She told the spies, "I know that Yhwh[1] has given you this land."[27]

Rahab gave the spies the military information they needed and, in return, asked for protection: "Please swear to me by Yhwh that you will show mercy to my family, as I have shown mercy to you."[28] The spies promised her that when they came to take the city, she would be protected if she gathered her family into her house and marked it with the scarlet escape cord in the window, reminiscent of the blood of the Passover lamb on the doorposts. Given this assurance, Rahab let the spies down the Jericho wall on the scarlet escape cord.

When the Hebrew people took the city of Jericho, Rahab and her family were spared as promised. She later married Salmon and became a mother in the royal line of Judah.

Rahab's inner truth gave her the power to open the gateway to the Holy One's purposes on earth. She also became a redeemer to her family and reflected divine love and mercy for all nations and all people.

---

[1] Yhwh—God, the Holy One

For Reflection or Discussion

1. Describe a time when you knew truth within and followed it even though it was difficult.
2. What can one do when there is a conflict between one's inner truth and the laws of one's country?

Ruth

The Power of Women United

The Book of Ruth and Matthew 1:5

Ruth of Moab walked with her sister-in-law, Orpah, beside their mother-in-law, Naomi, as she returned to Bethlehem. Ruth and Orpah had met and married Naomi's sons, Mahlon and Chilon, after the family had moved to Moab during a famine in Israel. But after ten years, Mahlon and Chilon and their father, Elimelech, had died, leaving the three women widowed without heirs, vulnerable in a patriarchal culture.

When there was no longer a famine in Israel, Naomi decided to return to relatives and friends in Bethlehem.

As Ruth and Orpah walked along the road toward Bethlehem, Naomi told them, "Return to your mother's house."[29] She blessed them and kissed them. Orpah went back, but Ruth stayed. She said, "Please don't ask me to leave you… Your people will be my people and your God, my God."[30]

Ruth had bonded closely with her mother-in-law, as she saw Naomi's faith sustain her through the death of her husband and sons. Ruth cherished this faith and wanted to stay with her and provide for her.

Soon after they arrived in Bethlehem, Ruth went to the fields to glean barley for Naomi and herself. As it happened, she worked in the fields of Naomi's relative Boaz. Boaz admired her devotion to Naomi and was very kind to her.

From Naomi, Ruth learned about the family-redeemer law: Ruth had the right to ask their nearest male relative to marry her to preserve her deceased husband's name, legacy, and land. Land was a sacred trust passed from generation to generation. Without children to inherit one's land, eternal promises and blessings were believed to be lost, and one's legacy was as lost as if one had never lived.

At Naomi's urging, Ruth went to Boaz and asked him to buy Naomi's land and become their family-redeemer. After consulting with a closer relative who declined, Boaz sealed the land transfer at the city gates in the presence of the elders.

Ruth and Boaz were married. With the birth of their baby, Obed, they redeemed the family's name, legacy, and inheritance of land. Obed became the father of Jesse and grandfather of King David.

Although no one could have foreseen the far-reaching consequences of Ruth's care and kindness, as women united,

Ruth and Naomi wrote an enduring legacy as family-redeemers, along with Boaz, in the patriarchal culture in which they lived.

For Reflection or Discussion

1. Consider the power of one vulnerable woman caring for another.
2. How might this power transcend international borders?
3. How might it bridge cultural gaps?
4. How might it redeem a sad legacy?

Bathsheba

From Rooftop to Palace

2 Samuel 11 and 12, 1 Kings 1 and 2, Matthew 1:6

Bathsheba was a newly married woman living in Jerusalem while her husband, General Uriah, was away at war. One evening, while Bathsheba was bathing on her rooftop, she received a summons to go to King David. She was told the king had seen her beauty and wanted to sleep with her. One does not refuse the order of a king, so Bathsheba complied. Weeks later, while her husband was still away at war, Bathsheba sent word to King David. "I'm pregnant."[31]

Soon thereafter, in the hope of covering up his actions, King David summoned Uriah home from battle, but Uriah was too honorable to sleep with Bathsheba while others were fighting and away from their families. So King David arranged for Uriah to be killed on the front lines of a fierce battle.

Bathsheba mourned. After her time of mourning, she and David were married. The child born to them became ill and died. Bathsheba grieved again. She wondered about the purpose of the painful circumstances that had taken her to the palace. As she listened for the Holy One's wisdom, she gained administrative skills and became a trusted advisor to King David. She also gave birth to four more children and reared them wisely.

Bathsheba, not King David, chose the next king. And she did not select the king's eldest son, as was tradition, but instead chose their son, Solomon, "the peaceful." King David honored her choice. And King Solomon honored his mother. He placed a throne for Bathsheba on his right, a position of power accorded the queen mother that superseded that of her son who was king.

When Solomon's elder brother Adonijah tried to usurp the throne by marrying his father's end-of-life companion Abishag, he first approached Bathsheba. Bathsheba wisely conferred with Solomon. Together they denied Adonijah's request and averted a coup.

Bathsheba's loyal son Solomon humbly asked the Holy One for leadership wisdom and was given wealth and fame besides. The nation enjoyed great peace during his reign. Solomon led in the building of the beautiful Temple, brought a united nation to its zenith, and became known throughout the world for his wisdom. But without Bathsheba, he would not have been born or become king—and none of these accomplishments would have taken place.

By listening to the Holy One's wisdom, Bathsheba moved beyond injustice and grief to integrity and a throne in her nation's palace. Her wise leadership redeemed a grievous sin in the nation's monarchy, led the nation to greatness, and restored its vision of Shalom.

For Reflection or Discussion

1. Recall a time you may have been given demeaning roles, labels, or limitations by others—or been treated as a sex object.
2. How might these experiences have led you to develop skills and abilities, to transcend cultural limitations, or to redeem the wrongdoing of others?
3. How might these experiences lead to accomplishing the Holy One's purposes in the world?

Three Women Architects

Women are the real architects of society.

—Harriet Beecher Stowe

Sheerah

Built Three Cities

1 Chronicles 7:20–24

Sheerah was from the tribe of Ephraim, the tribe from which Joshua came. She most likely lived in the ancestral land during the 400 years many of her relatives were in Egypt.

Sheerah's early life was marked by tragedy. During a cattle theft incident at Gath, two of her brothers were killed. Her family mourned for many days. When her parents gave birth to her brother, they named him Beriah, meaning "misfortune," to indicate hardship and tragedy in the family.

Sheerah was no stranger to life's difficulties, but as she listened for wisdom, she found the power within herself to turn life's hardships into strengths. And so, stone by stone, Sheerah built three cities in Ephraim near its border with the tribe of Benjamin: Upper Beth-horon, Lower Beth-horon, and the city that bears her name, Uzzen-sheerah.

Since one does not build a city alone, it is likely that besides construction skills, Sheerah was also a community builder—an organizer, motivator, and administrator. The strong boundaries of the cities she built continue to endure on one of the area's most historic roads.

Sheerah's work brings to mind the attributes of wise women in Proverbs 31: "She is up to the demands of labor and her limbs rise to meet the task… She enjoys the success that comes with hard work."[32]

As the builder of cities, Sheerah established firm boundaries and embodied the wisdom, strength, and courage that lead to peaceful living.

For Reflection or Discussion

1. How does one access the power within to turn hardships into strengths?
2. What are some ways to establish firm boundaries?
3. How do firm boundaries contribute to peaceful living?

Achsah

Inherited Land and Water

Joshua 15:16–19

Achsah—her name means "courageous"—was the daughter of Caleb, a "prince of Judah," and Joshua's early partner. As her father, Caleb, was leading the process of settling into the new land, he offered Achsah in marriage to the brave soldier who could conquer the city of Kirjath-sepher.

Achsah did not question the patriarchal custom of being offered by her father in marriage—especially if she was to be married to a hero. She happily married Othniel, but she was no trophy wife. Achsah knew her worth as a covenant bearer, and she wisely looked ahead to the needs of herself, her family, and her descendants.

Achsah knew a peaceful future for her family and country depended on everyone having a home, land to grow their own food and a water supply. Although the property was usually inherited by males and Achsah had three brothers, on the day of the wedding ceremony, she asked her father, Caleb, for land, and he gave her a share equal to that of her brothers.

Caleb further honored his daughter by asking, "Is there anything I can do for you?"[33] And Achsah answered, "You can give me a little present. Since you assigned me land in the arid Negev, you could give me a source of water as well."[34] So he gave her the upper and lower springs.

When Achsah's valiant husband, Othniel, later became the nation's leader and judge, Achsah's vision, courage, and sense of economic justice played a key role in the leadership and peace of the nation.

For Reflection or Discussion

1. How does a long-range vision of peace for one's family and country shape daily decision-making?
2. How does a vision of economic justice beyond tradition affect one's decisions and actions? How does it affect one's family and country?

Abigail

Redeemed Her Husband's Meanness

1 Samuel 25

Abigail was the beautiful wife of wealthy herder Nabal, while David was the scrappy leader of 600 men protecting flocks in the area. During the festive time of sheep shearing, David sent ten men to ask Nabal for food and supplies. But Nabal was drunk, surly, and mean. He insulted the men and sent them away.

Abigail was aghast when she heard what her husband had done. She knew his lack of hospitality for those who protected their flocks would bring on an attack. She knew what to do. She and her staff quickly baked 200 loaves of homemade bread and prepared mutton, parched grain, wine, raisins, and figs. Abigail led the way to deliver the supplies to David.

While on the way to David's camp, Abigail met him and 400 men who were coming to attack Nabal. She quickly dismounted and bowed before David. She apologized for her husband's actions and said, "I, your handmaid, missed seeing your messengers when they arrived."[35]

She continued, "Your highness, it is Yhwh who has restrained you from shedding blood and avenging yourself personally… When Yhwh carries out for you the promise of success and appoints you commander over Israel, you will not have this incident as a burden on your conscience."[36] Abigail begged David to receive the food and forgive Nabal's lack of hospitality. She praised David for his work and predicted his kingship.

David accepted her gift and said, "Return to your home in peace! For I have heard your wise counsel and granted your request."[37] Then she left.

The next morning, Abigail told Nabal what she had done. When he realized the danger of his actions to himself and his household, Nabal had a heart attack and fell into a coma. He died ten days later.

Abigail's wise diplomacy and prophecy were not lost to David. After Nabal's death, David asked her to be his wife. Abigail's wisdom and generosity helped transform him from a strong-minded and angry fugitive into a mature and generous king who led the nation to its zenith of unity and peace.

Abigail's peacemaking for her household sent ripples upward, shaped the monarchy, and moved a nation in paths of peace.

For Reflection or Discussion

1. How might simple acts of peacemaking at home send ripples upward?
2. What effect might everyday acts of generosity have on one's country? On the world?

Fearless Women

The best protection any
woman can have ...
is courage.

—Elizabeth Cady Stanton

Puah and Shiphrah

Midwives Who Stood before the King

Exodus 1

Puah and Shiphrah were chief midwives among the ancient Hebrew people who were living in the fertile area of the Nile River in Egypt. The Hebrew people had come to Egypt after a famine in their homeland and a redeeming relative had brought them there.

As the Hebrew people grew rapidly in numbers, the Egyptian king feared their potential to take over the country. So he appointed slave masters to oppress the people with hard labor.

When the Hebrew people continued to thrive, the king told Puah and Shiphrah, "When you assist the Hebrew women in childbirth, examine them on the birthing stool. If the baby is a boy, kill it. If it is a girl, let it live."[38]

The king's order conflicted with Puah's and Shiphrah's faith. They knew what they had to do. They risked their lives and ignored his order.

When the king learned Puah and Shiphrah were disobedient to his order, he summoned them to come before him. He bellowed, "Why have you let the male babies live?" Puah and Shiphrah replied politely, "These Hebrew women are different from Egyptian women; they are more robust, and deliver even before the midwife arrives."[39]

The king was no expert on midwifery. He had no response, so he let the midwives go.

As midwives, Puah and Shiphrah courageously facilitated the birth of the Holy One's purposes in the world, and they were blessed with families of their own.

For Reflection or Discussion

1. How does one decide when to conform and when to use civil disobedience?
2. What might be the far-reaching effects of one's decisions?

Jochebed and Miriam

Built a Floating Cradle and Made History

Exodus 2:1–10

After midwives Puah and Shiphrah refused to kill Hebrew boy babies at birth, the king commanded that all newborn Hebrew boy babies be thrown into the Nile River. Soon after this command, a Hebrew mother named Jochebed gave birth to a robust and healthy son. She chose faithfulness to the covenant over the king's orders, so she hid her baby for three months.

When she couldn't hide her baby any longer, Jochebed and daughter Miriam waterproofed a papyrus basket with tar and pitch. They put the baby in the water, inside the floating cradle among the reeds. Jochebed assigned Miriam to watch over the baby from a distance.

Soon the king's daughter and her maids came to the river to bathe. They heard the baby crying. The princess felt sorry for him. Miriam appeared from her hiding place and asked, "Do you want me to go and find a nurse for you among the Hebrews?"[40] When the princess said yes, Miriam brought her mother. The princess told Jochebed, "Take this child with you and suckle it for me, and I myself will pay you."[41]

When the child grew older, Jochebed took him to the palace, where the princess named him Moses because she said, "I pulled him out of the water."[42] The princess raised Moses as her son.

Because of Jochebed's and Miriam's actions, Moses learned both Hebrew and Egyptian cultures. This prepared him well for leadership in the Exodus.

The hands that rocked the cradle, made the cradle float, and watched over the cradle transformed a king's fear, oppression, and death sentence into a great blessing for a family, a nation, and the world. Jochebed and Miriam were fearless cradle rockers who changed history because, without their creativity and teamwork, there would have been no Moses to lead the Exodus and no Moses the Lawgiver.

For Reflection or Discussion

1. How might creativity and teamwork transform oppression into blessings where you live and work?

Jehosheba

Aunt Who Protected a Baby King

2 Kings 11:1–3, 2 Chronicles 22:10–12

Jehosheba, daughter of King Jehoram, was married to the high priest Jehoiada. She lived in the southern part of a divided kingdom during its decline. Her stepmother was Queen Athaliah, daughter of wicked King Ahab and Queen Jezebel of the Northern Kingdom.

After Jehosheba's father, King Jehoram, died, her half-brother Ahaziah reigned, and Athaliah held power as queen and queen mother. When Ahaziah was killed in battle, Athaliah seized the throne and promoted idolatry, immorality, and materialism as had her parents in the Northern Kingdom. Fearing any challenge to her power, Athaliah began killing off the royal family—even her own grandchildren.

When Jehosheba learned of her stepmother's plans for a bloody massacre, she acted to protect the spiritual leadership of their country and to continue the royal line. Risking her own life, Jehosheba stole away her baby nephew, Joash, who was not yet weaned and hid him with his nurse in a bedchamber in the Temple—a place where Athaliah was not likely to go.

Jehosheba kept little Joash safe through Athaliah's murderous rampage and six-year reign of terror. When Joash reached the age of seven, Jehoiada called civil and military leaders to the Temple, anointed Joash, and crowned him king.

Jehosheba's fearless actions played a key role in ending Athaliah's tyranny and preserving the royal line.

For Reflection or Discussion

1. What role does the care and protection of young children play in preserving a nation?
2. What are some ways women can survive and thrive in countries with oppressive leadership?

Jael

Took a Hammer

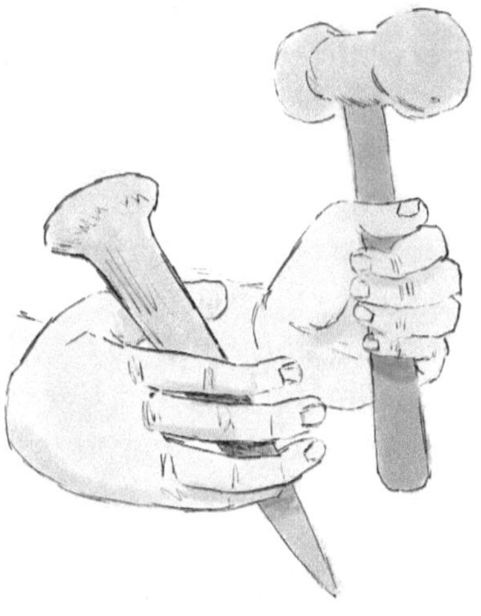

Judges 4:1–5:27

Jael was a Kenite/Midianite woman, a descendant of Moses' father-in-law, Jethro. The Kenites were metalsmiths who moved around a lot. At the time of this story, the Kenites were living in the Israelite area, caught in the middle of a conflict as Canaanite king Jabin and his chieftain Sisera threatened Israel.

During this time, Israel was ruled by a series of judges. The prophet Deborah was serving as the Israelite judge, and the military leader was Barak, who was hesitant to go into battle with Sisera. Barak consulted with Deborah, who prophesied, "I will go with you … but then you won't have the honor of victory from this battle—for Yʜwʜ will deliver Sisera into the hands of a woman!"[43]

The nomadic Kenites were weary of living in the middle of constant fighting. One day, as Jael drew water, a disheveled man stumbled into the Kenite camp and asked for a drink. She recognized him as Sisera, and she knew what she needed to do to put an end to the fighting and save lives.

Jael invited Sisera into her tent. Instead of water, she gave him milk and covered him with a blanket. Weary from battle and relaxed by milk, Sisera fell asleep. Whereupon Jael took a hammer and drove a tent peg through his temples.[2] Then she went to meet Barak and claim credit for defeating Sisera and putting an end to the war.

Jael's use of a hammer and tent peg to defeat an army of horses and chariots is immortalized in Deborah's Song of Victory, one of the oldest Hebrew songs of victory, similar to Miriam's Song of Triumph after crossing the Sea of Reeds.

For Reflection or Discussion

1. Describe a complex problem you see, and try to think of a simple solution.
2. What wisdom, gifts, opportunities, or tools do you have to resolve the problem?

---

[2] Editor's Note: Do not try this at home.

Hadassah/Esther

Captive/Queen Who Redeemed Her People

The Book of Esther

Hadassah was a young Jewish girl, an orphan and a refugee in Persia after her ancient Jewish homeland was invaded. She was adopted and reared by her cousin Mordecai, who worked at the Persian palace gates.

After Queen Vashti was dethroned, King Xerxes was searching for lovely young women who could become the new queen. Hadassah was urged by Mordecai to apply. Following months of preparation, the king chose Hadassah and crowned her as Esther, queen of an empire that reached from India to Ethiopia.

One day, Queen Esther received word from Mordecai that Prime Minister Haman had cast the pur to select a date when all Jews in Persia would be killed. Mordecai asked Esther to appeal to the king: "Who's to say?—you may have come into the royal court for just this moment."[44]

Esther knew if she went to the king without being invited, she could be killed. So she asked all Jews in Persia to fast and pray. She listened within for the Holy One's leading, and then she knew what to do. She said, "If I die, I die."[45]

As Queen Esther approached the king, he graciously welcomed her and offered her anything she wished up to half of the kingdom. She invited the king and Haman to come to a banquet that same day. At the banquet, the king repeated his offer, and Esther requested a second banquet. When the king made his offer a third time, Esther replied, "I ask you to spare my life, and the lives of my people."[46]

The king granted Esther's request. A massacre was averted, Haman was hanged instead of Mordecai, and a new law protected Esther and her people. Esther's courage transformed an act of hate into an act of divine deliverance, which is celebrated in the Feast of Purim each year.

For Reflection or Discussion

1. What are some situations of hate and violence that need transformation?
2. What are some qualities or actions that can transform hate into neighborly love and peace?

Assertive Women

Fight for the things that you
care about. But do it in a
way that will lead others to join you.

—Ruth Bader Ginsburg

Mahlah, Noah, Hoglah, Milcah, Tirzah

Sister Lawyers and Landowners

Numbers 26 and 27

Sisters Mahlah, Noah, Hoglah, Milcah, and Tirzah were in a difficult situation. The leaders of their fledgling nation were in the process of dividing ancestral land among the families of the twelve tribes. But in their culture, property was divided along patriarchal lines, so women by themselves had no property rights. Since their father, Zelophehad, had died and they had no brothers, the sisters would be disinherited and treated as if they did not exist.

But Mahlah, Noah, Hoglah, Milcah, and Tirzah had a keen sense of justice. They believed the Holy One's covenant included everyone. With no time to lose, they brought a lawsuit and took it straight to the top—the Tent of Meeting. In another break with custom and tradition, the sisters presented their case without a male advocate.

Mahlah, Noah, Hoglah, Milcah, and Tirzah stood before Moses, Eleazar the priest, the elders, and the whole assembly and stated, "Our father died in the desert ... and left no sons. But why should the name 'Zelophehad' disappear from the clan for lack of a son? Give us property equal to the share of our uncles!"[47]

Moses, Eleazar, and the elders conferred, but since there was no precedent for such a case, Moses took the matter directly to the Holy One, the highest Judge. The Holy One answered, "What the daughters of Zelophehad claim is right and just. You must allow them to inherit the share of property allotted to their uncles, and turn Zelophehad's inheritance over to them."[48] The Holy One also directed Moses to make this case a precedent for women's property rights.

Mahlah, Noah, Hoglah, Milcah, and Tirzah brought and won one of the earliest recorded lawsuits, which also made them landowners. They set a legal precedent that is still used today—and for good reason—because the rise and fall of nations is closely linked to the way women are treated.

For Reflection or Discussion

1. What might this story reveal about the connection between the Holy One and the power of women? Of sisterhood?
2. What laws regarding women's rights may need to be made more "right and just" today?

The Wise Woman of Tekoa Told a Good Story

2 Samuel 14

In the village of Tekoa, twelve miles south of Jerusalem, lived a woman who was known for her wisdom. One day, she was consulted by General Joab, who was concerned about incest, murder, and a banished son in the royal family. The woman was asked by Joab to go to a heartsick King David and tell a story that might help.

The woman knew she would be risking her life to go before the king, but she also knew divisions in the royal family threatened the well-being of the whole country. She listened for inner wisdom and knew what she had to do.

Before going to the king, the wise woman from Tekoa dressed in mourning clothes and looked as if she had been mourning for many days. When she came before King David, he asked what troubled her. She said, "Your majesty, I am a widow… I had two sons, but they came to blows in the fields, where there was no one to intervene; and one struck the other with a fatal blow."[49] She told King David the rest of her clan wanted to kill her remaining son, leaving her and her husband without name or heirs.

After King David promised protection for the woman and for her son, she asked, "Why then has the ruler … not returned his banished son? … Please devise a plan to let the one who has been banished no longer remain in exile!"[50] She offered the hope that by extending mercy to his own son, King David would bring reconciliation not only to his own family but to the nation.

Because of the woman's story—which King David knew was contrived—he brought back his banished son. The woman's story had called forth from within the king a new view of God's justice and care for unknown and banished people.

Although she remains nameless, the wise woman of Tekoa brought about reconciliation in the royal family and blessed the nation through her courage and storytelling.

For Reflection or Discussion

1. Has a wise friend ever told you a story that called forth a new perspective on justice—or injustice?

2. Have you ever been the friend who offered a new perspective?
3. How might peace within families and communities bring about peace in nations and the world?

The Shunammite Woman Reached Out to a Stranger

2 Kings 4:8–37, 8:1–6

A wealthy and influential woman of Shunem often invited Elisha to stay for a meal when he traveled through the village. Shunem was in the midst of rich grain fields on the route from Nazareth to Jerusalem where Elisha often traveled. After several visits, the woman told her husband, "I have come to believe that the person who stops for a meal is a prophet of God. Let us set up a small room on the roof with a bed, a table, a chair, and a lamp. Then he can stay here whenever he comes to see us."[51]

Out of gratitude for the couple's generosity, Elisha asked if there was anything he could do for them. They asked for nothing. But Elisha's servant Gehazi observed, "She has no son and her husband is old."[52] So Elisha told the woman, "About this time next year you will be holding a son in your arms."[53]

Elisha's prophecy came true, and the child was a joy to his parents. But one day, when he was in the fields reaping grain with his father, he cried, "My head! My head!"[54] An attendant carried the child to his mother, and he died in her arms.

Although the joy of her life seemed lost, a tiny flicker of hope stirred within the woman. She carried the child up and put him on Elisha's bed. Then, without telling anyone, she saddled a donkey and set out to find Elisha. She told her servant, "Lead on; and don't slow down for me unless I tell you."[55] When they found Elisha, the woman took hold of his feet and insisted he come with her.

Elisha went to the upper room in Shunem and found the boy dead on the bed. Elisha prayed. Then he stretched himself over the child mouth-to-mouth, eyes to eyes, hands to hands. After a while, the child's body grew warm. After he sneezed seven times and opened his eyes, Elisha put the child back in his mother's arms.

Sometime later, Elisha told the Shunammite woman to move her family to another land to avoid a seven-year famine. She believed Elisha and did as he said. But when she returned, most likely widowed, she discovered her house and land had been confiscated. She was not willing to accept this injustice, so she went directly to the ruler and asked for its return. Gehazi happened to be there and told the ruler this was the woman whose child Elisha had restored to life. The ruler instructed an official, "Give back everything that belonged to her, including all the income from her land from the day she left the country until now."[56]

The Shunammite woman, who offered hospitality to a stranger, recognized him as a prophet, and made a room for him in her home, experienced the Holy One's healing power, justice, and provision.

For Reflection or Discussion

1. Perhaps there was a time when you extended kindness to someone. How might the cycle of kindness have circled back to you?
2. Perhaps there was a time when you lost someone you loved and your joy seemed lost. How did you find a flicker of hope?
3. Perhaps there was a time you experienced injustice, and the Holy One sent someone to advocate for you. (If so, give thanks. If not yet, don't give up.)

Nurturing Women

The hand that rocks the cradle
is the hand that rules the world.

—William Ross Wallace

Nurse Deborah

Beloved Nurturer for Three Generations

Genesis 35:8

Nurse Deborah was Rebecca's caregiver. When Rebecca was born, Deborah was there to care for her. Deborah nurtured her into a strong and gracious woman whose offer to draw water for Abraham's steward and his ten camels identified her as the woman the Holy One had chosen to become Isaac's wife.

Deborah watched as Eliezer gave Rebecca a ring and two bracelets of solid gold and asked to meet with her family. She saw Rebecca's self-assured decision, willingness for adventure, and desire to become an heir to the Holy One's covenant. When Rebecca left with her family's blessing, Deborah went with her.

Deborah witnessed the joyous meeting of Rebecca and Isaac. She stood by Rebecca through twenty years of childlessness, and she was there when Rebecca became pregnant with twins and had turmoil in her womb. Nurse Deborah was there when the Holy One told Rebecca that "two nations are within your womb" and "the elder will serve the younger."[57] Deborah was the midwife for the birth of Esau and Jacob, and she nurtured them also.

Deborah saw Rebecca and Jacob deceive blind Isaac so Jacob could receive the firstborn's blessing. When Jacob had to flee because of Esau's wrath, nurse Deborah went with him. She became midwife and nurse to his family. She was the midwife when Rachel gave birth to Joseph. Deborah died before Rachel gave birth to Benjamin—which may be why Rachel died in childbirth.

Deborah was a beloved storyteller, midwife, and nurturer for three generations of covenant-bearers. When she died, the family buried her in a holy place—under the oak tree at Bethel where Jacob had received his vision of the well-traveled road between heaven and earth.

In the stories and genealogy of a patriarchal culture, Nurse Deborah was given one verse by which her life is remembered thousands of years later: "Then Rebecca's nurse

Deborah died and was buried under the oak near Bethel. Jacob called the place, 'Oak of Tears'."[58]

For Reflection or Discussion

1. In a patriarchal culture, Nurse Deborah was a single woman without children who nurtured a family through three generations—someone who might be seen as subservient or insignificant. Yet she was buried in a holy place, mourned by the family she served, and forever etched in Scripture.
2. How might Nurse Deborah's life speak to those who may think their life or work is insignificant?

Jedidah

Queen Mother Who Restored Leadership

2 Kings 22:1–2

Jedidah was queen while her husband Amon was king. Amon was the son of King Manasseh, who had done so much evil and covenant breaking that the Holy One pronounced judgment on the nation.

Jedidah watched sadly as her husband, King Amon, continued his father's evildoing. Two years into the reign, Amon was assassinated by his officials in the palace. The people of the land then killed Amon's assassins and made Amon and Jedidah's eight-year-old son, Josiah, king in Jerusalem.

In royal succession, the king's mother was the queen mother, whose power superseded that of the king. Jedidah served as a hands-on queen mother because Josiah was a child king. She nurtured and guided young Josiah in right paths and faithful leadership.

With Jedidah's guidance, "Josiah was just in the eyes of God."[59] He ordered the repair and restoration of the Temple. This led to the discovery of the Book of the Law, the nation's founding spiritual ideals. When the Book of the Law was read, young Josiah tore his clothes as he realized how far the nation had wandered. Influenced by Jedidah, he led the nation in repentance, education, and reform.

Married to a king who did evil, Jedidah used her role as queen and queen mother to change the direction of the nation. By guiding her son, Josiah, to lead justly, she transformed her husband's evil into good. Her influence restored the people's relationship with the Holy One and led the nation on the right path.

For Reflection or Discussion

1. Long before social media, Jedidah was an influencer. Consider the far-reaching power of a mother to influence children, community, and country.

Jerushah

Priestly Queen Who Bridged a Gap in Leadership

2 Chronicles 27:1–6, 2 Kings 15:33

Jerushah was the daughter of Zadok the priest and queenly wife of King Uzziah. Jerushah's husband, Uzziah, reigned for fifty-two years.

Uzziah secured the nation's borders, rebuilt towns that had been destroyed, built water towers and cisterns in the desert, and put people to work in fields and vineyards. He had a well-trained army and became very powerful.

But power and pride led to Uzziah's downfall. One day, he entered the Temple and attempted to burn incense, usurping the sacred task of consecrated priests. When the priests confronted Uzziah, he became angry. While he was raging, leprosy broke out on his forehead. He was quarantined in the palace until his death.

During the approximately ten years between Uzziah's shortened reign and the inauguration of their son Jothan as king, Queen Jerushah led the nation. Using the wisdom of her priestly upbringing, she taught Jothan the relationship between obedience and blessing and held her son to high standards. Under Jerushah's leadership, "Jothan grew strong, living a life that was resolutely obedient before Yhwh."[60] Jothan did what was right, as his father Uzziah had done, but unlike Uzziah, he did not attempt to usurp the sacred task of priests in the Temple.

Jerushah's wise leadership bridged the gap between the reign of her husband and her son. As the daughter of a priest, as a queen, and as a queen mother, she became a bridge of blessing for her family and nation.

For Reflection or Discussion

1. Jerushah's story brings to mind the many times women need to bridge the gap when the sudden absence of someone else thrusts them into a leadership position. How does the daily living of sacred values prepare one to bridge gaps in leadership?

Unnamed Women

If you think you are too small
to make a difference,
you haven't spent the night
with a mosquito.

—African Proverb

The Bahurim Woman With a Mystery in Her Well

2 Samuel 17–19

There was trouble in the royal family. King David's son Absolom had gathered a large army to usurp the throne. King David covered his head and left the palace barefoot and weeping. On his way into hiding, David and his supporters passed through the village of Bahurim on the eastern slope of the Mount of Olives, between Jerusalem and the Jordan

River. King David's loyal subjects wept as he passed through their village.

His loyal supporters in Jerusalem sent out messengers with vital information about Absolom's plans. The messengers knew Absolom's informants were hot on their trail, so they found a home in Bahurim and hid in the well. The woman of the home covered the mouth of the well with a cloth and scattered grain over the cloth.

When Absolom's men asked the woman if she had seen two men running past, she replied, "They crossed over the brook,"[61] sending the pursuers in the wrong direction. David's messengers emerged from the well and reached David in time to warn him to quickly cross the Jordan River for safety.

The next day, Absolom's hair was caught in a tree, and he was killed. His followers scattered, and the uprising ended. David, although deeply saddened, returned to the palace in Jerusalem.

In the midst of an ordinary day, the Bahurim woman with a mystery in her well turned the tide of a royal power struggle. And though it ended sadly, her actions helped restore the rightful leader of her country. Her simple actions and five well-timed words are etched in Scripture as a wellspring of peacemaking wisdom.

For Reflection or Discussion

1.   Recall a time a simple action or a few simple words changed the outcome of a situation or brought peace.

The Wise Woman of Abel
Expert Conflict Manager

2 Samuel 20

After Absolom's rebellion, a troublemaker named Sheba started a revolt against King David. When pursued by David's commander-in-chief Joab, Sheba took refuge in the fortified northern city of Abel. Joab's army built a siege ramp and began battering the walls of the city.

A wise woman in the city called down from inside the walls, "Listen! Listen! I must talk to Joab!"[62] Joab came and listened. The woman said, "In the old days ... people used to settle their disputes by coming to us. Our town is one of the most peaceful and loyal in Israel. She is one of Israel's mother-cities, and you seek to kill her! Would you swallow up Yhwh's own possession?"[63]

Joab said it was not his intent to destroy Abel but to deal with Sheba, who had threatened King David and had taken refuge in the city. He said, "If you hand him over, we will withdraw from the city."[64]

The woman discussed Joab's offer with leaders of the city. Upon her advice, the people cut off Sheba's head and threw it over the wall. Joab and the soldiers promptly withdrew from the city.

The wise woman of Abel took charge of her city's safety when it was threatened. She spoke truth to power and initiated the process of conflict resolution. She presented the case in terms of spiritual truth and involved the city's people in the decision. Her quick action and diplomacy prevented all-out war and destruction and brought about a peaceful outcome.

For Reflection or Discussion

1. When trouble threatens the peace of many, what are some ways to resolve a conflict before it escalates?
2. Who are some wise women you know who are skilled at resolving conflict?

The Widow with Oil
When Little Became Much

2 Kings 4:1–7

A widow whose deceased husband had been a friend of the prophet Elisha was left with debts she could not pay. She came to Elisha and said, "My husband, your disciple, has died… Now his creditors are coming to take away my two boys as slaves."[65]

Elisha said, "How can I help you? Tell me what you have in your house." The woman replied, "I have nothing there at all—except a little oil."[66]

Elisha told the woman, "Go around your neighborhood and ask all your neighbors for empty jars, as many as you can. Then go inside and shut yourself in with your sons. Pour oil into all the jars, and as each is filled, put it to one side."[67]

Risking her neighbors' skepticism, the woman went around the neighborhood to ask for empty jars. To her surprise, when hearing of her request, neighbors brought empty jars to her home.

The woman went inside, closed the door, and poured oil into the jars. When oil from her small pot had filled all the jars, the oil stopped flowing. Elisha told her to sell the oil and pay her debts. She and her sons were able to live well on what was left.

The widow who was on the brink of despair found within herself the courage and faith to transform scarcity into abundance and make visible the divine economy where little is much. She enjoyed daily provision, relief from debt, and the freedom of her two sons. Her story continues to inspire, bless, and empower all who hear it.

For Reflection or Discussion

1. Reflect on an experience that at first seemed impossible. What happened next?
2. How does one move from fear-of-not-enough into a spiritual economy of abundance?
3. How might the instructions to "go around your neighborhood" and "go inside" inform one's journey of faith?
4. What do you have in your house?

The Wise Little Maid

Brought Healing to Higher-Ups

2 Kings 5:1–19

A young Israeli girl who had been taken captive by the Arameans became the maid of Commander Naaman's wife. Naaman was a mighty warrior and highly esteemed officer, but he had leprosy. One day, the little maid told her mistress, "If only Naaman would see the prophet who is in Samaria. He would cure Naaman's leprosy."[68]

When Naaman's wife told him what the little maid had said, Naaman consulted the King of Aram, who sent a letter to the King of Israel to arrange Naaman's visit. The King of Israel tore his clothes because he thought it was a setup. But the prophet Elisha assured the king, "Have Naaman come to me and he will learn that there is a prophet in Israel."[69]

When Naaman and company arrived at Elisha's home, Elisha sent his servant with a message for Naaman to wash seven times in the Jordan River. Naaman was insulted that Elisha had sent his servant, and he was angry at the humiliating treatment. He had expected Elisha to greet him personally and make the leprosy disappear, whereupon he would give Elisha lavish gifts. In time, Naaman's servants calmed him. They suggested that dipping in the Jordan River was a simple thing to do and urged him to give it a try.

After the seventh dip, Naaman's leprosy was gone. He went back to thank Elisha and offer gifts, but Elisha would not accept them. Naaman left with some Israeli dirt to kneel on when he prayed to the Holy One who had healed him.

The healing of powerful Naaman came about because of the wise little maid, who was not concerned with power struggles between nations. She showed higher-ups the impartiality of divine healing power and the way to peace among nations.

For Reflection or Discussion

1. While leaders saw life through the lenses of power struggles and suspicions and protocols and snubs, the wise little maid's concern for the health of her master won the day, and leaders bowed before the Holy One. How might one's worldview change when looking through a child's eyes at the Holy One's love and care for everyone?

The Widow of Zarephath

An Amazing Jar of Flour and Jug of Oil

1 Kings 17:7–24

A widow was gathering sticks near the city gates of Zarephath, between Tyre and Sidon, north of Israel. The drought was severe. She was almost out of flour and oil when the prophet

Elijah, on the run from Queen Jezebel, asked, "Could you bring me a little water in a jar for me to drink? … And please bring me a piece of bread."[70]

The widow knew Elijah was a prophet. She meant to be kind, but she had no bread. So she blurted, "As YHWH lives, I don't have any bread—only a handful of flour in a jar and a little oil in a jug. I am gathering a couple of sticks to take home and make a meal for myself and my child. We will eat it—and then we will die."[71]

She fed Elijah first, as he asked. She received and believed his promise: "The jar of flour will not be used up and the jug of oil will not run dry until the day YHWH makes it rain on the land."[72] And it remained so throughout the drought.

Later, when her child became ill and stopped breathing, she scolded Elijah: "What do you have against me, man of God? Did you come to remind me of my sin and kill my child?"[73] Elijah carried the child to an upper room and cried out to the Holy One to restore the child's life.

The child began breathing again. As the woman held her child in her arms, she told Elijah, "Now I know that you are a man of God, and that the word of YHWH is truly on your lips."[74]

Although she was not from Israel, the widow of Zarephath believed the Holy One's prophet and sustained him through a difficult time. Her scarcity was turned into abundance, and she bore witness to divine power over death. Her story has empowered people through the ages, showing divine love and blessings are for all people.

For Reflection or Discussion

1. A desperate widow in a famine and a hungry prophet on the run from one who sought to harm

him. What made the story of two desperate people turn into a win-win situation?

2. Think of a situation that seems desperate to you. Create some possible endings to the story. How might the situation work for the good of all?

Prophetic Women

Reverence for Yhwh is the
beginning of wisdom;
and knowledge of the Holy
One is understanding.

—Proverbs 9:10

Naomi

Prophet Who Lamented

The Book of Ruth

Naomi lived in Bethlehem with her husband, Elimelech, and their sons, Mahlon and Chilon. Her life was full.

When there was a famine in Bethlehem, the family moved to the nearby country of Moab. While there,

Elimelech died. Mahlon married Ruth, and Chilon married Orpah. But after ten years, Mahlon and Chilon also died. Naomi's life became empty—without wealth, without husband, children, or grandchildren.

As she journeyed back to Bethlehem alone, her daughter-in-law Ruth refused to leave her, vowing, "Where you go I will go, and where you lodge I will lodge. Your people will be my people, and your God, my God."[75]

When Naomi and Ruth arrived in Bethlehem, Naomi lamented to the women, "I was filled to the brim when I departed, but YHWH has brought me back empty… YHWH has passed sentence upon me and Shaddai has brought me to ruin."[76]

As a widow without children, Naomi depended on her widowed daughter-in-law Ruth for survival. Ruth gleaned grain in the fields all day during the harvest, unknowingly working in the field of Boaz, who was Naomi's husband's relative. When Naomi learned where Ruth was gleaning, she told Ruth about the levirate law, in which Boaz could become their kinsman-redeemer by marrying Ruth.

After conferring with a closer relative, arrangements were made at the city gate for Ruth and Boaz to be married. The couple was blessed with baby Obed.

As Naomi held her grandson in her arms, the women of Bethlehem said, "Your daughter-in-law, who loves you and has proven better than seven of your own children could have been, has given birth to him."[77] Naomi's life was full again.

Naomi's life journey was woven through times of emptiness and fullness. In her sorrow and sadness, she was a prophet who lamented. As she cried out to God, she released her sadness and created an empty place for the Holy One to fill. In the end, her arms were filled with a grandchild, Obed, who became the grandfather of David, the shepherd-king who began the royal line.

For Reflection or Discussion

1. What is the glue that held together Naomi's times of emptiness and fullness?
2. When Naomi experienced trouble and loss, she did not keep silent or keep a stiff upper lip. She lamented. What was her lament to the women of Bethlehem?
3. As Naomi held baby Obed, what wisdom did the women of Bethlehem glean from her life's journey?
4. Optional: Write a lament (see Appendix A) about a time of emptiness, grief, or pain in your life.

Hannah

Prophetic Mother Who Asked of the Holy One

1 Samuel 1 and 2

After the ancient Hebrew people were in their Promised Land and their leaders Moses and Joshua had died, they were a loose confederacy ruled by a series of judges. Near the end of this time, Hannah lived with her husband Elkanah in the village of Ramah. Elkanah, a priest, had another wife, Peninnah, who bore him children, but Hannah was barren.

Peninnah, jealous of Hannah's favor with Elkanah, taunted Hannah. This was especially difficult for Hannah, a woman of deep faith in a culture that believed the Holy One opened and closed wombs. She was very sad during the family's annual trips to worship at the Tent of Meeting in Shiloh.

One year, Hannah wept all the way to Shiloh and would not eat. She went to the Tent of Meeting and poured out her anguish and grief. She prayed silently, her lips moving, and made a vow. "YHWH Omnipotent, look with pity on your handmaid. Don't forsake me. Remember me. If you will give me a child, a male, I will dedicate him to you. For all the days of his life, he will neither drink wine nor liquor, and no razor will ever touch its head."[78]

The priest Eli believed Hannah was drunk and chided her. Hannah replied, "Oh no! It isn't that! I am a woman with a broken heart! … I have been pouring out my heart before YHWH… I am simply pouring out my feelings of grief and misery."[79]

In due time, Hannah conceived and gave birth to a son, whom she named Samuel. She prayed again: "My heart delights in YHWH… YHWH lifts the weak from the refuse dump … and promotes them to seats of honor… Now YHWH will endow the ruler with strength and exalt the head of the anointed one."[80] Hannah loved and nurtured Samuel and provided his early spiritual training. When Samuel was of age, she fulfilled her vow and brought him to live and serve at the Tent of Meeting.

At the Tent of Meeting, Samuel was nurtured into a great prophet and circuit-riding judge. He upheld the nation's divine covenant through crises and transitions. He preserved the nation's spiritual heritage, leading it from a confederacy to a monarchy and from the Bronze Age to the Iron Age. He anointed the nation's first two kings, Saul and David.

Because of Hannah's prayer and faithfulness to her vow, the Holy One shaped her child, Samuel, into a great spiritual leader and blessed her with more children. Hannah's laments, prayers, and prophetic wisdom brought blessings to her family, her nation, and the world.

For Reflection or Discussion

1. How might prayers of lament, petition, thanksgiving, and prophetic vision sustain women today through oppression, scorn, and the feeling of being forsaken by the Holy One?

Deborah

Prophet under a Palm Tree

Judges 4 and 5

After the ancient shepherding people settled into their Promised Land and their leader Joshua died, everyone did what was right in their own eyes. When the people strayed from their covenant, the Holy One allowed surrounding nations to attack. A series of judges or governors led them through these ups and downs.

Deborah was one of the judges. She was a homemaker and wife of Lapidoth, keeper of the tabernacle lamps. Her prophetic wisdom made her a sought-after counselor. People came to Deborah's palm, where she held court and offered discernment and guidance.

After the Hebrew people had been oppressed by King Jabin of Canaan for twenty years, Jabin's army, led by General Sisera, approached the Hebrew people with its 900 ironclad chariots. The people were fearful. Deborah sent for Barak and instructed him, "Yhwh, the God of Israel, commands this: 'You are to lead 10,000 Israelites from Naphtali and Zebulun to Mount Tabor. I will lure Sisera, Jabin's commander, with his chariots and troops to the Kishon River and you will defeat him there.'"[81]

Barak was fearful and would not go into battle unless Deborah went with him. So she said, "Very well, I will go with you... but then you won't have the honor of victory from this battle—for Yhwh will deliver Sisera into the hands of a woman!"[82] So Deborah went with Barak, providing military strategy and encouragement. The Holy One caused a storm of sleet and driving rain to disable Sisera's soldiers, horses, and chariots. Armed with moral courage and trust in the Holy One, the Israelite army prevailed against the well-trained and well-armed Canaanite army. Because of Deborah's leadership, the Israelites again put their trust in the Holy One rather than in idols and weapons, and the fledgling nation enjoyed forty years of peace.

As prophet and counselor, judge and deliverer, Deborah's unyielding faith led her to the height of political power. One of the earliest martial songs was composed about her, including "Village life died a lonely death until you rose up, Deborah, the great mother of Israel."[83] Deborah continues to be an example of the power of women's spirituality and prophetic leadership.

For Reflection or Discussion

1. Perhaps there is a prophet-woman you know who offers true spiritual discernment and guidance. How has her wisdom helped you or someone you know?
2. Perhaps you are a prophet-woman whose discernment and guidance provide leadership for your community and beyond. Lead on!

Huldah

Prophet Who Inspired a Renewal

2 Kings 22–23, 2 Chronicles 34–35

Huldah was at her home near the palace in Jerusalem, where her husband was keeper of the king's wardrobe. One day, Hilkiah, the high priest, and top aides came to her door with a scroll and some questions.

Hilkiah had been gathering money for the repair of the Temple when he stumbled upon a Scroll of the Law given by Moses. He tended the money first and then had someone read the scroll to King Josiah. When Josiah heard the words of the scroll, he tore his clothes and wept. He realized how far his country had strayed from its covenant and the painful consequences that would soon occur. King Josiah told Hilkiah, "Go and ask Yhwh for me ... about the contents of this book that was found."[84] Whereupon Hilkiah went directly to Huldah.

Huldah was known for her wisdom and spiritual perception. She examined the scroll carefully and then told Hilkiah, "This is what Yhwh says: 'I will bring disaster on this place and on its people, according to everything written in the book ... because they abandon me and burned incense to other gods and provoked me to anger by all the idols made with their hands.'"[85] As a special message for King Josiah, she said, "Tell the ruler of Judah, who sent you to ask God, 'Because your heart was responsive and you humbled yourself before God ... and because you tore your clothes and wept in my presence, I have heard you... Your eyes will not see all the disaster I am going to bring on this place.'"[86]

After Hilkiah left, Huldah wondered sadly why the high priest, the official spiritual leader of the country, had not recognized the scroll and was not familiar with its contents. Was the high priest more focused on fundraising than on spiritual leadership? Was this why the people had forsaken their covenant and worshipped idols?

After hearing Huldah's prophecy, King Josiah turned to the Holy One with all his heart and soul and strength. He destroyed the idols in the land. He called the leaders together and held a celebration of the Passover, such as had not been held since the days of Samuel. He began an education program and led the people in renewing their sacred covenant.

From her home near the palace, the prophet Huldah had inspired a national spiritual renewal.

For Reflection or Discussion

1. Sometimes the most influential leaders are not in official positions. Perhaps you know someone without a title or salary whose wisdom and vision have blessed your life and the lives of others.

Appendix A

The Anatomy of a Lament

Over half the Psalms are laments—heart cries of people in distress seeking divine help. The ancient Hebrew people knew they were not to pretend all was well when it wasn't. It was their privilege and duty to cry out to God when they were in distress. Lamenting kept their relationship with God open and honest. The lament transformed their distress, moving them from one way of orientation, through disorientation, and to reorientation—a closer walk with God.

There are some basic parts to a lament. Not all may be present in each lament or in the order below, but most laments contain many of these seven components:

1. Naming God: "My God, my God…"
2. Pouring out the complaint, even exaggerating.
3. The petition—telling God what is needed or desired.
4. Telling God what is at stake in granting the request, such as God's honor.
5. Asking for vengeance on the enemy who is responsible for the problem—putting vengeance into God's hands rather than one's own.

6. A time of waiting expectantly in silence: Selah.
7. Something has changed, and there is an expression of gratitude, praise, and thanksgiving for answered prayer.

Bibliography

Deen, Edith. *All of the Women of the Bible*. New York: Harper & Row, Publishers, Inc. 1955.

Priests for Equality. *The Inclusive Bible*. Lanham, MD: Rowman and Littlefield Publishers, Inc., 2007.

Endnotes

(All scripture quotes, unless otherwise noted, are from *The Inclusive Bible*.)

[1] Genesis 12:2–3
[2] Genesis 17:15
[3] Genesis 17:5
[4] Genesis 18:12
[5] Genesis 18:13
[6] Genesis 21:6
[7] Genesis 16:8
[8] Genesis 16:8
[9] Genesis 16:11
[10] Genesis 16:9–10
[11] Genesis 16:14
[12] Genesis 21:17–18
[13] Genesis 24:18
[14] Genesis 24:19
[15] Genesis 25:22
[16] Genesis 25:23
[17] Genesis 31:14–15
[18] Genesis 38:16
[19] Genesis 38:16
[20] Genesis 38:17
[21] Genesis 38:18
[22] Genesis 38:24
[23] Genesis 38:25
[24] Genesis 38:26
[25] Joshua 2:3
[26] Joshua 2:4–5
[27] Joshua 2:9
[28] Joshua 2:12

29 Ruth 1:8
30 Ruth 1:16–17
31 2 Samuel 11:5
32 Proverbs 31:17–18
33 Joshua 15:18
34 Joshua 15:19
35 1 Samuel 25:25
36 1 Samuel 25:26, 30–31
37 1 Samuel 25:35
38 Exodus 1:16
39 Exodus 1:19
40 Exodus 2:7
41 Exodus 2:9
42 Exodus 2:10
43 Judges 4:9
44 Esther 4:14
45 Esther 4:16
46 Esther 7:3
47 Numbers 27:3–4
48 Numbers 27:6–7
49 2 Samuel 14:5–6
50 2 Samuel 14:13–14
51 2 Kings 4:9–10
52 2 Kings 4:14
53 2 Kings 4:16
54 2 Kings 4:19
55 2 Kings 4:24
56 2 Kings 8:6
57 Genesis 25:23
58 Genesis 35:8
59 2 Kings 22:2
60 2 Chronicles 27:6
61 2 Samuel 17:20
62 2 Samuel 20:16
63 2 Samuel 20:18–19
64 2 Samuel 20:21
65 2 Kings 4:1
66 2 Kings 4:2
67 2 Kings 4:3–4
68 2 Kings 5:3

69 2 Kings 5:8
70 1 Kings 17:10–11
71 1 Kings 17:12
72 1 Kings 17:14
73 1 Kings 17:18
74 1 Kings 17:24
75 Ruth 1:17
76 Ruth 1:21
77 Ruth 4:15
78 1 Samuel 1:11
79 1 Samuel 1:15–16
80 1 Samuel 2:1, 8, 10
81 Judges 4:6–7
82 Judges 4:9
83 Judges 5:7
84 2 Kings 22:13
85 2 Kings 22:16–17
86 2 Kings 22:18–20

About the Author

Celia M. Hastings has a master's degree in religious education from Western Theological Seminary in Holland, Michigan. She is the author of *A Bible Survey Curriculum for Adults (The Wisdom Series)* and *The Undertaker's Wife: Wisdom and Musings; Life in a Small-Town Funeral Home.*

She lives with her retired undertaker husband in northern Michigan, where she writes weekly articles for a local newspaper. She is the mother of one son and nana of three grandsons. Besides writing, she enjoys savoring chocolate morsels and assembling jigsaw puzzles while listening to music.